NATIONAL AUDUBON SOCIETY® POCKET GUIDE

A Chanticleer Press Edition

Richard Spellenberg
Professor of Biology
New Mexico State University

Ann H. Whitman
Editor

Contents

How to Use This Guide

Wherever there is soil that has not been covered by pavement, plants manage to establish themselves and produce flowers. Even in cities, wildflowers are a pleasure to find and identify.

Coverage

This new guide covers 80 of the most common native wildflowers of the East—species that anyone is likely to encounter. Our geographical range is bounded by the Atlantic Ocean on the east, and on the west by the 100th meridian, extending from Edwards Plateau in Texas northward through Oklahoma and westward through eastern Colorado, Wyoming, and Montana, and Canada, along the eastern foothills of the Rocky Mountains. A companion volume covers flowers west of the Rockies.

Organization

This easy to-use guide is divided into three parts: introductory essays; illustrated accounts of the flowers; and appendices.

Introduction

As a basic introduction, the essay "Identifying Flowers" suggests some guidelines for discovering the identity of an unfamiliar wildflower. "The Form of a Flower" describes the basic structure of various families of flowers. Black-and-white drawings illustrate different kinds of flowers, leaves, and clusters.

The Flowers	This section contains 80 color plates arranged visually, according to the color and shape of the bloom. Facing each illustration is a description of the most important characteristics of each flower, including its geographical range and habitat. The introductory paragraph describes look-alikes and relatives, among other topics. A black-and-white drawing of each plant supplements the photograph.
Appendices	Featured here is "Families and Their Members," an alphabetical listing of all the flower families in the guide, with the names and page numbers of the species represented.
A Word of Caution	Many wildflowers are edible, and some have been used for centuries as medicines, aphrodisiacs, or food. The interesting histories of these plants have been included here, but this book is not a guide to edible plants. There are many toxic species in North America, and some can be fatal; to the inexperienced eye, these poisonous plants may be difficult to tell from innocuous look-alikes. Do not risk making a mistake; do not eat any plant you find growing in the wild.

Identifying Flowers You will easily learn to identify many wildflowers by paying attention to three general kinds of features: where the plant grows, its vegetative characteristics, and the characteristics of the flower. Once you learn what questions to ask yourself, you will gain a general understanding of all the plants on the continent.

Location Where is the plant found? Botanical exploration of North America is reasonably complete, and there are few surprises left. If you think you have identified a plant, but the range description does not match, the identification is probably not correct, although the plant may be a close relative of the wildflower described. Some species have very exacting habitat requirements.

Stems and Leaves What are the characteristics of the stems and leaves? Features of the stem contribute to the general aspect, or habit, of the plant. Does the stem branch? If so, does the branching occur only at the top or the bottom? Is the plant tall? Short? Short and matted? Are all the leaves and flowers attached at one point near the ground (rosettes)?
Are the leaves divided (compound) or not (simple)? If simple, what is their shape? Are the edges plain, lobed,

or toothed? If the leaves are compound, are they palmate (shaped like a hand)? Pinnate (like a feather)? More than once pinnately compound? How are they placed on the stem? Is there only one at a point on the stem (alternate)? Two at a point (opposite or paired)? More than two (in rings or "whorled")?

Flowers For the beginner, the symmetry of the flower and nature of the petals are the most important aspects to study. Is the blossom actually composed of many small flowers surrounded by a ring of green bracts? (If so, the plant is probably a member of the daisy family.) As you look at the flower, is it radially symmetrical, like a wheel? Or is it bilaterally symmetrical—that is, can it be divided only down the center into two equal halves?
How many petals are there? Are they joined or separate? If joined, do they form a tube, trumpet, funnel, bowl, or saucer? Are petal lobes evident?
The position of the ovary—the part of the flower that produces the fruit—can be important in identification. Is the ovary in the center of the flower, with all the other parts attached at its base? Or is the ovary inferior, with the parts all attached at the top, making the ovary visible from the side of the flower?

9

The Form of a Flower

The way a flower looks has a significance beyond natural beauty: Form and color are important in successful reproduction. A flower's development must be precisely coordinated and timed to mesh with the activities and abilities of its animal pollinators. For these reasons, the form of a flower tends to be complex, precise, and stable. The flower parts—the stamens, sepals, petals, and ovaries—must function together precisely, while the color and odor attract pollinators. The nectaries—and often the pollen as well—provide incentives for insects or birds to visit the flowers.

Generally speaking, very similar flowers are members of closely related groups—species, genera, and families. A knowledge of family characteristics provides a general familiarity with wildflowers throughout temperate North America. Learning a few very large families, such as the buttercup, pea, or sunflower (daisy) family, gives the satisfaction of recognizing something familiar and eases the burden of trying to distinguish among a thousand or more species.

Evolution Plants have evolved at different rates. In general, more advanced species or families have fewer individual parts (stamens, ovaries, petals, and sepals), and those parts

10

are joined to some degree. Fairly primitive families, such as the buttercup family, have separate sepals, separate petals, many stamens, and many separate ovaries. Members of the more advanced rose family have similar flowers, but the bases of the petals, the sepals, and the stamens are all joined to form a cup, or hypanthium, around the ovary or ovaries.

One of the most advanced families is the sunflower family. This huge group may give the beginner some trouble, because what appears to be a flower is actually a head made up of hundreds of tiny flowers; the "petals" surrounding the head are called rays. Each of the tiny flowers that make up the head has an inferior ovary that produces a single seed.

Fusion   Sometimes, similar flower parts are fused; this adaptation encourages pollination by visiting insects or birds. Members of the morning glory, waterleaf, and borage families, for example, all have five petals that are fused; in the morning glories, the petals form a funnel, while in the other two groups, the flower clusters form "fiddle-necks."

The Number of Parts   Many wildflowers have just a few of each kind of flower part. The mustard family, for example, is easy to recognize by its four sepals, four petals, six stamens (four long ones and two short ones), and an ovary that is divided into two chambers by a papery partition. Members of the evening primrose family also have four sepals and four petals, but they differ in having either four or eight stamens; the ovary is inferior.

Lilies have three sepals (which look like petals in some species), three petals, six stamens, and an ovary with three chambers. Members of the iris family have three stamens and bear the ovary beneath all the other parts of the flower. Like many families, the mallows have five petals and five sepals; the stamens are joined at the base in the middle of the flower, and look like a small shaving brush.

Symmetry   Many flowers have radial symmetry, like a wheel: You can draw an imaginary line through the center, and the same structure will be evident on each side of the line. Other flowers have responded to animal pollinators by developing bilateral symmetry—a left and a right side. The pea family is a large group of bilaterally symmetrical flowers. Members of the family are easy to recognize; they have a large upper petal, two smaller side petals, and two lower petals that are joined like the keel of a

12

boat. There are ten stamens; nine are usually joined, and the uppermost one is then independent.

Some flowers with fused petals are also bilaterally symmetrical. The members of the mint family are easy to recognize; they have a four-sided stem, opposite leaves, and (usually) a minty odor; the distinctive flowers have two or four stamens, and the ovary divides into four hard segments, or nutlets. Most of the showy members of the snapdragon family have four pollen-bearing stamens (others have two or five); the ovary forms a capsule with two chambers.

The orchids are highly advanced flowers with three petal-like sepals and three petals; the lower one of the three is always different from the two upper ones. The central complex of one or two stamens is joined to the style (the narrow part of the female portion of the flower above the ovary); the ovary itself is inferior.

There are thousands of wildflowers in North America, and no single book can include them all. By learning to recognize family characteristics, however, it is possible to gain a solid basis that will serve you well as you become more expert at flower identification.

Parts of a Flower

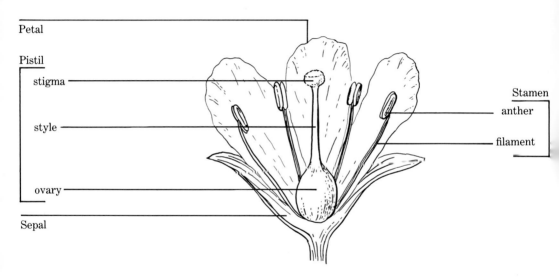

Petal

Pistil
- stigma
- style
- ovary

Sepal

Stamen
- anther
- filament

Disk Flower

Ray Flower

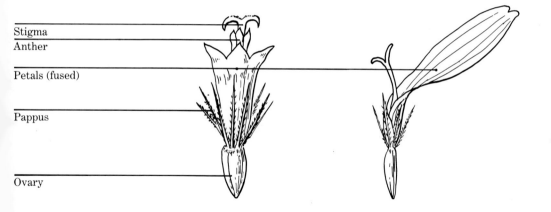

Stigma

Anther

Petals (fused)

Pappus

Ovary

Composite Flower

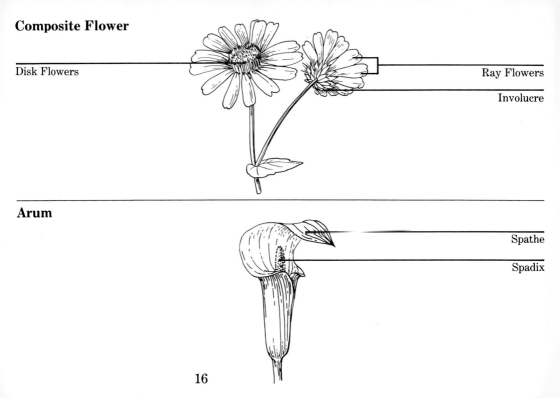

Disk Flowers

Ray Flowers

Involucre

Arum

Spathe

Spadix

16

Iris

Standard (petal)

Petal-like Style

Crest

Fall (sepal)

Pea Flower

Banner

Wing

Keel

17

Cluster Types

Raceme

Spike

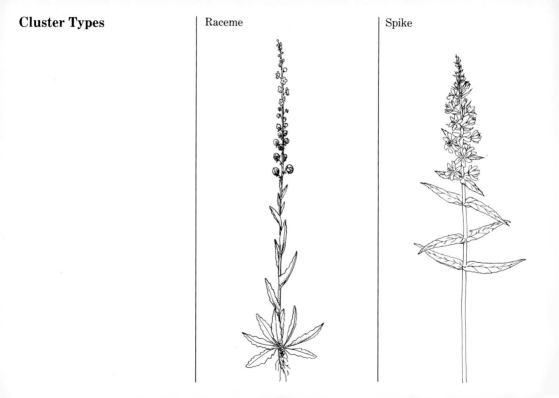

Corymb

Umbel

Cyme

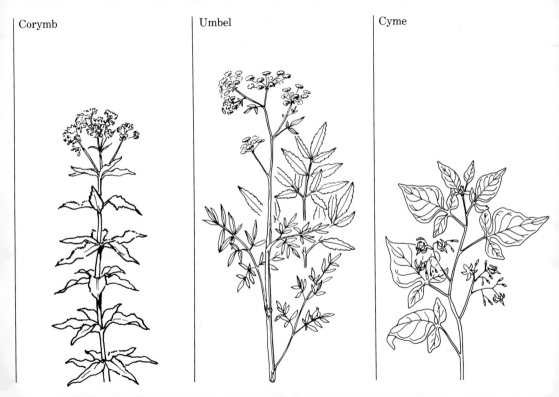

Leaf Types

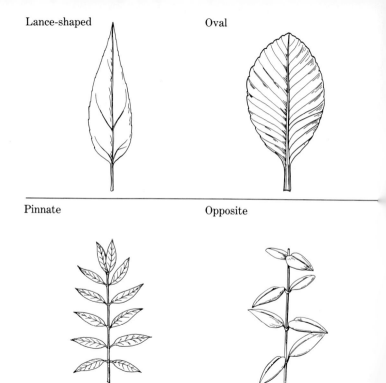

Lance-shaped

Oval

Pinnate

Opposite

Toothed

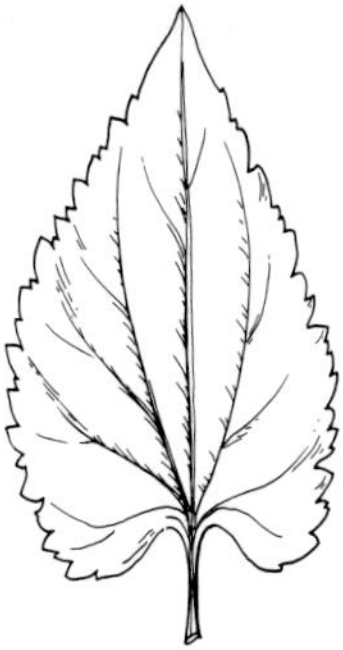

Lobed

Palmate

Alternate

Clasping

Basal

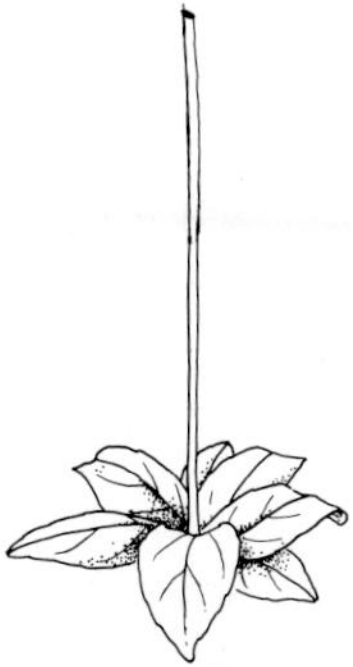

The Flowers

Fragrant Water Lily *Nymphaea odorata*

In some cultures, water lilies are considered a symbol of perfection, beauty, and purity because the blossoms float on the surface, untouched by the muddy water. These flowers are not true lilies but form their own family, which includes the sacred lotus of ancient legend. The Fragrant Water Lily has a spongy leafstalk with four main channels to carry oxygen from the surface down to the large stems (rhizomes) buried in the muck. This species blooms only from early morning until about noon; the Small White Water Lily (*N. tetragona*), with flowers about half the size, is open in the afternoons. Both bloom from June to September.

Identification Aquatic plant with large, fragrant white or pink flowers and round, flat leaves. Height: Submerged leafstalks may be several feet long. Flowers 3–5″ wide, with many pointed petals intergrading with numerous yellow stamens. Leaves 4–12″ across, reddish beneath.

Habitat Quiet water.

Range Throughout the East.

24

Pasqueflower *Anemone patens*

The name Pasqueflower refers to this plant's nature of flowering early in the spring, near Passover and Easter, and to the purity of its delicate, pastel flowers. The genus name is an old Greek word for wind, and many species of *Anemone* are called windflowers. In early legend of Native Americans, the Pasqueflower was a herald of spring, and, with its shaggy head of feathery seeds, also a symbol of old age. The state flower of South Dakota, it blooms from April to June.

Identification   A silky-hairy stalk with a solitary white, pastel blue, or purple flower growing from a cluster of deeply cut leaves. Height: 6–16″. Flowers about 2½″ wide, with 5–7 petal-like sepals and no petals. There are numerous stamens. Leaves at the base, hairy and repeatedly divided into narrow segments, with stalks; immediately below the flower is a circle of 3 stalkless leaves. Fruit seedlike, with long feathery "tails" forming a shaggy head.

Habitat   Prairies and grassy areas.

Range   NW. Canada east to Wisconsin and Michigan, south through Illinois and Missouri to Texas; also in the West.

26

Bloodroot *Sanguinaria canadensis*

This delicate spring flower, a member of the poppy family, opens in the sun and closes at night, often partly enfolded in its single basal leaf. The stout underground stem bleeds red when cut open, and was used by Native Americans to dye baskets and clothing and as war paint. It was also called Red Puccoon; "puccoon" is traceable through Native American words to their word for blood. The sap was also used as an insect repellent and to cure coughs, colds, and skin diseases. Bloodroot blooms from March to May.

Identification A solitary white flower with a golden center blooms on a smooth stalk growing beside a single leaf, which often curls around the stalk. Height: 4–10″. Flower to 1½″ across, with 8–10 white petals, and many golden stamens at center. Sepals 2, falling as the flower opens. Leaf bluish green, round, 4–7″ long, palmately scalloped into 5–9 lobes.

Habitat Rich woods.

Range E. Canada south to Florida, west to E. Texas, north to North Dakota.

28

Partridgeberry *Mitchella repens*

This creeper is a distant relative of the tropical coffee
and gardenia plants. It has round, shiny leaves similar to
those of a hedge plant, box (*Buxus*), and it is sometimes
called Running Box. An attractive ground cover,
Partridgeberry has two kinds of flowers: Some plants
have flowers with long stamens and short pistils, others
just the opposite, helping to ensure cross-pollination. As
the fruit of each flower matures, it fuses with that of its
neighbor, producing a "twin berry" or "two-eyed berry."
This species blooms in June and July.

Identification	A trailing herb forming mats, with tubular, fragrant white flowers in pairs. Height: Creeping, only about 1″ tall, but with stems to 1′ long. Flowers ½–⅔″ long, tubular; with 4 spreading petal lobes, hairy-fringed on the inside. Leaves roundish, ½–¾″ long; shiny green with white veins. Fruit a double berry, usually red (rarely white).
Habitat	Dry or moist woods.
Range	E. Canada south throughout the East.

30

Large-flowered Trillium *Trillium grandiflorum*

Trilliums are among the most popular wildflowers. Because they bloom in early spring, at about the time the robin arrives from its southern winter stay, they are sometimes called wake robins. Various species have been used by Native Americans in many ways: for food, to alleviate ailments, as an aphrodisiac, and to bring ill-fortune to an enemy. The greens may be cooked and eaten, but rootstocks often die if the leaves are not present to recharge the stored nutrients each year. The Large-flowered Trillium, a member of the lily family, blooms from April to June.

Identification   A large flower, waxy white at first, becoming pink, growing on an erect stalk above a circle of 3 broad leaves. Height: 8–18″. Flowers 2–4″ wide with 3 wavy-edged petals; the 3 branches of the stigma are straight, not tapered, and directly on top of the ovary. Leaves 3–6″ long; broad and pointed.

Habitat   Rich woods and thickets.

Range   Ontario, Quebec, W. Maine, and New Hampshire south to Georgia, west to Arkansas, and north to Minnesota.

32

Common Strawberry *Fragaria virginiana*

The fruit we enjoy is actually the central portion, or receptacle, of the strawberry flower. The hard, seedlike ovaries, when fertilized, secrete a hormone stimulating the growth of the receptacle; if the flower is not fertilized, the "berry" will be malformed. Commercial strawberries are hybrids whose parentage usually includes the Common Strawberry and a South American race of the western Beach Strawberry (*F. chiloensis*). The Common Strawberry has the seedlike achenes sunken in pits on the fruit; the similar Wood Strawberry (*F. vesca*), also found in the East, bears them on the surface. Both bloom from April to June.

Identification   Long-stalked, 3-part leaves and white flowers growing from runners. Height: 3–6″. Flowers ¾″ wide, with 5 roundish petals and many stamens. Leaves in 3 parts; leaflets broad, 1–1½″ long, toothed, with terminal tooth usually shorter than those along sides. Seedlike fruit sunken within fleshy red cone formed by receptacle.

Habitat   Open fields and edges of woods.

Range   Throughout much of the United States and S. Canada.

34

Wood Anemone *Anemone quinquefolia*

Along woodland borders in the early spring, loose patches of Wood Anemones appear, each stem bearing a single, starlike white flower. By its many stamens and ovaries in the center, this species can be recognized as a member of the buttercup family; as such, it is a relative of the larkspurs, columbines, and buttercups. The Wood Anemone is closely related to the Lance-leaved Anemone (*A. lancifolia*), which is generally more than 8″ tall and has coarse teeth on the leaves nearly to the base. In both species the sepals are white and petal-like, and true petals are lacking. Both bloom from April to June.

Identification Open patches of white flowers with 5 petal-like parts on top of a single stem and a ring of 3 palmately divided leaves with toothed edges. Height: 4–8″. Flowers about 1″ across with 4–9 sepals. Leaves 3, in a ring beneath the flower, each divided into 3 or 5 segments about 1¼″ long. Fruit seedlike, in a dense cluster.

Habitat Open woods, clearings, and thickets.

Range Quebec to W. New York, south to North Carolina, and locally in Ohio and Kentucky.

36

Spotted Wintergreen *Chimaphila maculata*

Spotted Wintergreen is conspicuous in winter or summer because of the white and green mottled leaves. The genus name, from Greek *cheima* ("winter") and *philein* ("to love"), like the common name, indicates that the plant stays green the during winter. Also called Striped Wintergreen, this species appears to increase both vegetatively and by seed after light wildfires. A slightly taller relative, Pipsissewa (*C. umbellata*), has shiny, dark green leaves that lack the mottling. Both species bloom from June to August.

Identification	Nodding, fragrant, white or pinkish flowers are held in a cluster above a ring of green and white mottled leaves. Height: 3–9″. Flowers about ⅔″ wide; 5 roundish petals recurved, exposing 10 stamens. Leaves ¾–2¾″ long, lance-shaped; striped with white along the midvein. Fruit a round, brown capsule; lasts all winter.
Habitat	Dry woods.
Range	S. Ontario to S. New Hampshire, south to Georgia, west to Arizona, north to Illinois and Michigan.

Dutchman's Breeches *Dicentra cucullaria*

The generic name of this delicate spring flower derives from Greek for "two-spurred"; knowing this, it is easy to see the resemblance between the Dutchman's Breeches and the pink flowers of the related Wild Bleeding Heart (*D. eximia*). These flowers are pollinated by certain early bumblebees that have a proboscis long enough to tap the nectar in the spur. Another relative, Squirrel Corn (*D. canadensis*) also has heart-shaped flowers. A member of the poppy family, Dutchman's Breeches blooms in April and May.

Identification   Clusters of fragrant, pantaloon-shaped white flowers overtop soft, much-divided leaves. Height: 4–12″. Flowers ¾″ long; 2 outer petals with inflated spurs (the "legs" of the "pantaloons"), and 2 smaller inner petals. Sepals—little flaps by the stalk—drop off. Leaves 3–6″ long, divided into many narrow leaflets.

Habitat   Rich woods.

Range   Nova Scotia and Quebec, south through Appalachians to Georgia, west to Alabama, Missouri, E. Kansas, and North Dakota; also in Oregon.

40

Indian Pipe *Monotropa uniflora*

These waxy white plants seem mysterious, even ghostly, hidden in their shady woodland haunts. They are somewhat translucent and lack the least bit of green. The early green ancestors of Indian Pipe grew in rich, shaded woods, where they developed an association with a root fungus, decreasing their dependence on sunlight. Later descendants of these plants absorbed all nutrients from the duff, and were saprophytes—totally dependent on the fungus and capable of living in the deep shade. Indian Pipe blooms from June to November; it turns black when picked, and it cannot be transplanted.

Identification	Translucent white stems, hooked at top, bearing 1 flower, usually white, sometimes salmon-pink. Height: 3–9″. Flower ½–1″ long, with 4–5 petals. Leaves are small scales.
Habitat	Rich deep woods with ample duff.
Range	Throughout much of North America; south to Central America.

Smooth Solomon's Seal *Polygonatum biflorum*

The arched stems, orderly leaves, and hanging flowers of this woodland plant convey a dignified grace. There are several suggestions for the origin of the name Solomon's Seal. Solomon, king of the Hebrews nearly 3000 years ago, was the son of David. A modern story suggests that the six-pointed flower represents the Star of David, for a long time known as "Solomon's seal." More commonly, the leaf scars on the rootstock are said to resemble the seal of Solomon, and a very old version reports that the plant has value in "sealing" wounds. Hairy Solomon's Seal (*P. pubescens*) has hairy leaves on veins beneath the leaves. Both species bloom from May to July.

Identification Arching stems with few (often 2) greenish-white flowers hanging from the point where leaves join the stem. Height: 8–36″. Flowers ½–⅔″ long; bell-shaped, with 6 petal-like parts. Leaves 2–6″ long; stalkless, lance-shaped or broader. Fruit a round, blue-black berry.

Habitat Dry to moist woods and thickets.

Range Connecticut and New York south to Florida, west to Texas, north to Nebraska and S. Ontario.

44

Mayapple *Podophyllum peltatum*

The flower of this species superficially resembles that of the apple, and the plant blooms around the month of May, giving rise to the common name. The ripe, golden-yellow fruits are edible and are sometimes used to make interesting jelly, but the rest of the plant is poisonous. The root was once used for medicinal purposes, and the plant is sometimes called Mandrake because of the properties of the root and its shape, which is like that of the superstitiously feared, but also medicinally valued, true Mandrake from the Old World. Mayapple blooms from April to June.

Identification   A solitary, nodding white flower blooms in the angle between a pair of large, deeply lobed leaves. Height: 12–18″. Flowers 2″ wide, with 6–9 waxy white petals and twice as many yellow stamens. Leaves to 1′ wide. Fruit yellow, to 2″ long, lemon-shaped.

Habitat   Rich woods and damp, shady clearings.

Range   S. Ontario and W. Quebec south to Florida, west to Texas, and north to Minnesota.

Arrowhead *Sagittaria latifolia*

The shape of the leaves of this common aquatic plant gives it the name Arrowhead. There are several related species with similar leaves, which must be distinguished by technical differences of the flower and the seedlike fruit. Still other species have very narrow leaves—in some almost grasslike—but share this species' habitat and distinctive white flowers. In the muck, the plants produce starchy, edible tubers that float to the surface when the mud is disturbed; they are a favorite of ducks and muskrats, and for this reason, the species is also called Duck Potato. Arrowhead blooms from July to September.

Identification Aquatic plant with emergent, arrowhead-shaped leaves; flowers in rings of 3 on the stem, each with 3 white petals. Height: 1–4′. Flowers nearly ¾″ wide. Leaves 2–16″ long, varying from narrow and unlobed to broader, and arrowhead-shaped. Fruit seedlike, in globose heads; fruit has winglike edges, but no winglike ridges on face.

Habitat Stream and pond margins, marshes, and swamps.

Range Throughout much of North America.

Moth Mullein *Verbascum blattaria*

The broad, spreading petals and the fuzzy stamens in the center resembling the antennae of a moth give this plant its common name. There are several species of mulleins in our range; originally Old World plants, they were introduced to the New World with colonization and have spread rapidly. Those species that grow in the wild have apparently always been weeds; a few others are grown in gardens. Moth Mullein, a member of the snapdragon family, blooms from June to September.

Identification	A long, open cluster of yellow or white flowers with 5 rounded petals, marked with brownish purple on the back. Height: 2–5′. Flowers about 1″ wide. Stamens 5, with orange pollen sacs and violet hairs on the stalk. Leaves 1–5″ long; coarsely toothed; clasping the stem; triangular to lance-shaped.
Habitat	Old fields and roadsides.
Range	Throughout much of temperate North America.

Prairie False Indigo *Baptisia leucantha*

These plants are called "indigo" because many contain a blue dye that resembles indigo; the pigment becomes noticeable as the plants blacken upon drying. True indigo is derived from a tropical plant, *Indigofera*, in the same family as this one. Species of *Baptisia* readily hybridize in the wild; it is with these plants that botanists first demonstrated that hybrids otherwise difficult to detect could be distinguished by chemicals in the leaves. This species, which is also called White Wild Indigo, blooms from May to July.

Identification Bushy perennial with smooth leaves and pealike white or cream flowers held in stiffly erect clusters; stems covered with a whitish bloom. Height: 2–5'. Flowers to 1" long, in spires to 1' long. Leaves palmately divided into 3 oblong segments, each 1–2½" long. Fruit a pod about 1" long, drooping from a long stalk that protrudes from the calyx; pod turns black when dry.

Habitat Prairies, open woods, and waste places.

Range Ontario south to Ohio and Mississippi, west to Texas, north to Nebraska and Minnesota.

52

Death Camas *Zigadenus nuttallii*

"Camas" comes from a Native American word meaning "bulb." Bulbs of many species in the lily family were important in early diets, including those of the wild onions (*Allium* spp.) and the Wild Hyacinth (*Camassia scilloides*). But the similar-looking bulbs of the Death Camas have long been feared; highly toxic, they cause severe nausea, prostration, coma, and even death. Related species occur throughout much of North America; the collector of wild foods should avoid any onionlike plant with white or cream-colored flowers and without the characteristic onion odor. Death Camas blooms in April and May.

Identification	A nearly leafless stem rising from basal leaves and bearing a branching cluster of numerous, starlike greenish-white flowers. Height: 1–2½′. Flowers about ½″ wide, with 6 petal-like parts, each with an egg-shaped greenish gland at the base. Leaves about ½″ wide, to 2′ long. Bulb has a papery outer jacket.
Habitat	Prairies and open woodlands.
Range	Tennessee west to Kansas and Texas.

Catnip *Nepeta cataria*

The silly antics that this plant provokes in cats are caused by a chemical called nepeta lactone, which is a natural insect repellent. Catnip is therefore useful in a garden to protect other plants from insects, but the plant may invite neighborhood cats to trample delightedly in the flowerbed. Catnip was introduced to North America from Europe. It can be recognized as a typical member of the mint family by its minty odor as well as by the small white flowers, which produce a hard fruit with four seedlike segments, and by the four-sided stem. Catnip blooms from June to September.

Identification   Densely hairy, branched plant with terminal clusters of bilateral whitish flowers with purplish spots. Height: 1–3′. Flowers ½″ long, strongly bilateral; upper lip 2-lobed, hoodlike, lower lip 3-lobed, scooplike. Stamens 4, protruding. Leaves opposite one another on the stem, 1–2½″ long, triangular, coarsely toothed, paler underneath. Fruit in 4 seedlike segments.

Habitat   Roadsides, waste places, pastures, and barnyards.

Range   Throughout much of temperate North America.

56

Water Hemlock *Cicuta maculata*

Water Hemlock looks like parsnip, but it is the most violently toxic plant in North America. A small amount may cause death after severe and painful convulsions. Leaves unknowingly collected with other edible plants have caused poisoning, so the collector of wild plants must know these plants well. Learn the characteristic umbrellalike flower cluster (umbel) of the carrot family; avoid the plants until you are sure of your knowledge. Water Hemlock blooms from June to September.

Identification   Smooth, erect, branched plant with purplish-streaked stem bearing dome-shaped, open clusters of small white flowers. Height: 3–6'. Flowers about ⅛" wide, with no bracts at base of main branches of flower cluster. Leaves to 1' long, doubly divided; leaflets sharp-pointed and toothed, with veins ending in notches between teeth. Roots partitioned into stacked chambers, visible in dissected roots.

Habitat   Wet places in meadows and thickets; also in swamps.

Range   S. Ontario to Nova Scotia, south to Florida, west to Texas, and north through Missouri to Canada.

58

Queen Anne's Lace *Daucus carota*

Often called Wild Carrot, this ancestor of the carrot also has an edible root, but it is a small one and hardly worth the effort. The flower clusters served 18th-century English courtiers as "living lace," hence its common name. From a distance, Queen Anne's Lace can be easily confused with Yarrow (*Achillea millefolium*), but the latter is a member of the sunflower family, and has a flat-topped cluster of tiny white flower heads; it never has a purple or brown flower in the center. Queen Anne's Lace blooms from May to October.

Identification   A lacy, flat-topped cluster of tiny white flowers, usually with one dark reddish-brown flower in the center; divided leaves along stalk. Height: 1–3'. Flower cluster to 6" across; divided bracts with slender segments at junction of flower clusters. Older clusters resemble a bird's nest. Leaves 3–8" long, fernlike, repeatedly divided into narrow segments. Fruit seedlike, with tiny barbed prickles on every other rib.

Habitat   Dry fields and waste places.

Range   Throughout temperate North America.

60

Oxeye Daisy *Chrysanthemum leucanthemum*

This is the common white and yellow daisy of the fields. In Anglo-Saxon, *daeges eye* meant "day's eye," and referred to the little English lawn daisy, which closes at dusk and opens again in the morning. Oxeye Daisy, a member of the sunflower family, belongs to a genus of about 100 species; many of these and their hybrids are popular late-season ornamentals. Introduced from Europe, probably as a garden plant, the Oxeye Daisy is disliked by farmers because it is weedy and can produce an undesirable flavor in the milk of cows that graze it. It blooms from June to August.

Identification   Central yellow disk surrounded by white rays; leaves are dark green. Height: 1–3′. Flowerheads 1–2″ wide; disk has depression at center. Leaves coarsely toothed or pinnately lobed, up to 6″ long; upper leaves shorter.

Habitat   Waste places, meadows, pastures, and roadsides.

Range   Throughout much of temperate North America; less common in the South.

Common Fleabane *Erigeron philadelphicus*

"Bane," a word of dark meaning, is commonly a part of plant names; it comes from the Anglo-Saxon *bana*, for "destroyer." Such plants, which are often toxic, were once thought to ward off evil animals. Fleabane was used to rid places of fleas; the plant juice was applied as a lotion to the body, and dried stalks and leaves were burned in a pot as a fumigant. Plants in the genus *Erigeron* belong to the sunflower family; they tend to flower earlier than their relatives. Common Fleabane—also called Philadelphia Fleabane—blooms from April to August.

Identification Small flower heads with numerous, very slender white to pink rays around a yellow disk; leaves on the stem "clasp" it at their notched bases. Height: ½–3′. Flower heads ½–1″ wide with 150–400 rays. Bracts around the head tend to line up more like fence pickets than to overlap like shingles. Leaves may be toothed; basal leaves to 6″ long; stem leaves smaller.

Habitat Thickets, fields, and open woods.

Range Throughout much of temperate North America.

64

Common Dandelion *Taraxacum officinale*

Originally a weed, the Common Dandelion came to North America as a garden plant. The leaves may be eaten fresh or cooked, and the roots can be cooked; a wine made from the heads was once said to bring summer into the house during even the worst blizzard. There are different races: Some are adapted to grow in shade among taller weeds, and others do best as short plants in hard-trodden sod. Now a mostly unloved weed, Common Dandelion blooms from March to September.

Identification | Slender, hollow stalks bear a single bright yellow flower head with strap-shaped flowers, longer toward the edge than in the middle; stem produces milky sap. Height: 2–18". Flower heads 1–1½" wide. Bracts under flower head narrow and pointed; outer ones bent backward. Leaves basal, narrow, 2–16" long; deeply and irregularly toothed on the edges. Fruit seedlike, with a stalked, feathery white "parachute."

Habitat | Fields, roadsides, and lawns.

Range | Throughout most of temperate North America; less common in the extreme SE. United States.

Black-eyed Susan *Rudbeckia hirta*

The black eye is, of course, the dark central disk of this member of the sunflower family, but nobody knows who Susan was. Coloring roadsides and fields in late summer, this bright and gay wild plant is the state flower of Maryland. There are several species in the genus, but this is the only one in the region to have no crown of bristles or scales at the top of the seedlike fruit. Livestock usually avoid Black-eyed Susan, which can be toxic. It blooms from June to October.

Identification	Coarse, rough-stemmed plant with daisylike flower heads composed of showy golden-yellow rays surrounding a dark brown central button. Height: 1–3′. Flower heads 2–3″ wide; hemispheric central disk ½–¾″ wide, surrounded by 8–21 rays. Leaves rough-hairy, lance-shaped, 2–7″ long; narrow or broad; lower ones lack teeth, upper ones with fine or coarse teeth, all with 3 prominent veins; leafstalks winged. Fruit seedlike, without bristles or scales at top.
Habitat	Roadsides, fields, prairies, and open woods.
Range	Throughout much of the East; sporadic westward.

68

Jerusalem Artichoke *Helianthus tuberosus*

Jerusalem Artichoke is related to Common Sunflower (*H. annuus*), a popular gigantic-headed garden flower and supplier of seed and oil. "Jerusalem" is a corruption of the Italian *girasole*, meaning "turning to the sun"; the heads of both species follow the path of the sun through the sky. Jerusalem Artichoke has been cultivated for centuries for its edible tuber, which may be boiled or roasted or eaten raw, and which contains no starch. In 1805, Lewis and Clark dined on the tubers, prepared by a squaw, in what is now North Dakota. Jerusalem Artichoke blooms from August to October.

Identification Stout, rough-branching stems bear large golden flower heads. Height: 5–10′. Flower heads to 3″ wide, with 10–20 ray flowers; narrow and spreading bracts beneath the head. Leaves 4–10″ long; lance- or egg-shaped (but pointed), opposite on the lower part of the stem, alternate above, with winged stalks and 3 main veins.

Habitat Areas with moist open soil.

Range Throughout the East and west to Rockies.

70

Tall Goldenrod *Solidago altissima*

The nearly 60 species of goldenrod in the East, all members of the sunflower family, have showy clusters of small yellow heads and seedlike fruits with slender, usually white, bristles on top. They are conspicuous and bloom when people are suffering from hay fever—for which malady they have been blamed. However, the irritation is caused by ragweed (*Ambrosia* spp.), a less conspicuous wind-pollinated plant. Common and showy, Tall Goldenrod blooms from August to November.

Identification Small yellow flower heads on outward-arching branches form a pyramidal cluster atop a grayish, downy stem. Height: 2–7'. Flower heads about ⅛" long, with 10–17 rays, each ⅛" long or less; more rays than disk flowers. Leaves lance-shaped, those at the base smaller than those on the mid-stem and soon withering. Mid-stem leaves to 6" long; 3-veined, slightly rough above, hairy beneath; sometimes toothed. Fruit seedlike, hairy.

Habitat Thickets, roadsides, and clearings.

Range S. Ontario and Quebec to New York, south to Florida, west to Arizona, north to Kansas and North Dakota.

Goatsbeard *Aruncus dioicus*

"Goatsbeard" probably refers to the long, loose cluster of flowers. This plant is in the rose family and should be distinguished from the very similar member of the saxifrage family, False Goatsbeard (*Astilbe biternata*). One must examine the tiny flowers closely to be sure of the distinction. *Aruncus* has three ovaries close to one another, but not joined. *Astilbe* has two sections to the ovary, joined except for the tips; also, on its leaves, the terminal leaflet is usually both lobed and toothed, instead of just toothed. Goatsbeard blooms from May to July.

Identification   Tall plants with very small, whitish flowers arranged along branches of a large, open, feathery cluster. Height: 3–6′. Flowers about ⅛″ wide, with 5 petals and sepals. Plants are either male or female; if male, flowers have many stamens; female flowers have 3 ovaries. Leaves to 15″ long, divided 2–3 times into toothed leaflets, each 2–5″ long.

Habitat   Woods and ravines.

Range   Pennsylvania south to Georgia, west to Alabama and Kentucky.

74

Common St. Johnswort *Hypericum perforatum*

This European species is a common weed. Introduced in the East in 1793, it spread rapidly, and made land in some areas worthless until it was brought under control in the 1940's. Because this species blooms around Midsummer's Day, it was once dedicated to the Teutonic sun god Baldur. On Midsummer's Eve, supernatural beings were believed to be abroad; this plant, gathered then and hung in doorways or carried in pockets, was thought to ward off spirits all year. In the Christian calendar, June 24 became the feast day of St. John the Baptist, and Baldur's yellow flowers became St. Johnswort. It blooms from June to September.

Identification   Starlike, bright yellow flowers bloom in a round-topped cluster; stems branched and leafy, especially near the top. Height: 1–3′. Flowers 5-pointed stars, about 1″ across; petals may have black dots near tips. Stamens many, clustered into 3–5 bunches. Leaves paired, ½–1½″ long; elliptical, with many tiny, dark, translucent dots.

Habitat   Fields, roadsides, and waste places.

Range   Throughout much of temperate North America.

76

Charlock *Brassica kaber*

This common species is very similar to the wild mustards from which our familiar condiment is produced. It can be told from Black Mustard (*B. nigra*) by the three prominent veins on each half of the fruit; Black Mustard has just one vein. The genus has done more than flavor frankfurters; rutabaga, turnip, curled kale, pak-choi, and kohlrabi are all *Brassica* species. Cabbage, Brussels sprouts, cauliflower, and broccoli are all varieties of one species. Charlock blooms from May to July.

Identification Widely branched plants with deeply lobed leaves and narrow clusters of small yellow flowers near the top. Height: 8–32″. Flowers about ½″ wide, with 4 petals; 4 long stamens, 2 short ones. Leaves 1½–3″ long; lower ones coarsely toothed or sometimes lobed, the upper progressively smaller. Fruit a cylindrical, usually hairless pod ascending at a sharp angle to the stem, with a seed-containing body ½–¾″ long; topped by a seedless beak the same length or smaller.

Habitat Fields and waste places.

Range Nearly throughout temperate North America.

78

Fringed Loosestrife *Lysimachia ciliata*

Loosestrifes, for the most part, can be recognized by their starlike yellow flowers and (like all good members of the primrose family) by the stamens attached at the middle of the petal base, not alternating with the petals. The genus is named for Lysimachus, a Macedonian general renowned for "loosing strife" on the battlefield; he is credited with discovering that the plants pacify quarrelsome beasts of burden, checking their bad tempers. This species blooms from June to August.

Identification An erect stem, sometimes branched, bearing stalked yellow flowers arising from the bases of opposite leaves; leafstalks fringed with spreading hairs. Height: 1–4′. Flowers ¾″ wide; usually pointing outward or downward; 5 broad petals, minutely toothed across the rounded end and tipped with a small, sharp point; 5 fertile stamens alternate with 5 small sterile ones. Leaves lance- or egg-shaped and pointed, 2½–5″ long.

Habitat Damp woods and thickets; also floodplains.

Range Quebec and Nova Scotia south to Georgia and west to New Mexico and British Columbia.

Evening Primrose *Oenothera biennis*

All the evening primroses, as their name suggests, open their flowers in the evening, in a rapid process of jerks and starts that is easily observed over a short period of time. Soon after opening, the flowers are visited by hummingbird moths, and each flower closes the next morning forever. The plant, a biennial, takes two years to complete its life cycle. Its basal leaves become established the first year, and flowering occurs in the second. There are 18 species in the East, and all but two have yellow flowers. This species blooms from June to September.

Identification Lemon-scented, large yellow flowers bloom at the top of a leafy stalk; stem hairy, often purple-tinged. Height: 2–5′. Flowers 1–2″ wide, with 4 broad petals and 4 sepals bent sharply back, arising from the top of a long floral tube; stamens 8. Leaves 4–8″ long, lance-shaped, with shallow teeth. Fruit an oblong capsule, about 1″.

Habitat Fields and roadsides.

Range Throughout the East; also in the West.

82

Downy False Foxglove *Aureolaria virginica*

Downy False Foxglove and true Foxglove (the source of digitalis) are both in the snapdragon family, but they are not closely related. The origin of the name foxglove is uncertain, but the flowers are about the right size and shape for the paws of a fox. There are several species in the East, all with tubular, bilateral yellow flowers. Downy False Foxglove and some relatives are partly parasitic on oak roots. This species blooms from June to August.

Identification   At the top of a downy stem is an open cluster of funnel-shaped yellow flowers, each flower growing singly in the angle formed by a bract and the stem. Height: 1–5′. Flowers 1″ wide, slightly bilateral; the opening surrounded by 5 broadly rounded petal lobes; individual flower stalks beneath each flower ⅛″ long or less (sometimes lacking). Leaves 2½–5″ long, paired on the stem, downy; lower ones pinnately lobed. Fruit a pointed, egg-shaped capsule, about ½″ long and hairy.

Habitat   Dry, open woods.

Range   New Hampshire to N. Florida, west to Louisiana, and north to Michigan.

84

Butter-and-eggs *Linaria vulgaris*

A beautiful wildflower and a noxious weed, Butter-and-eggs is native to Europe, where it was once believed a cure for jaundice, piles, and conjunctivitis; it was also pretty in the garden. Brought to America around 1800, it immediately began its conquest; this durable weed is deceptively delicate but will grow anywhere. Like the related snapdragon, it has a "mouth" that opens when the flower is squeezed. The orange path on the lower lip guides insects to the nectar within. The equally unwelcome Dalmation Toadflax (*L. dalmatica*) has lance-shaped leaves and slightly larger flowers. Butter-and-eggs blooms from May to October.

Identification   Bilateral yellow flowers, with downward-pointing spurs, angled upward near the top of a leafy stem. Height: 1–3′. Flowers about 1″ long; upper lip 2-lobed, the lower lip 3-lobed and with orange ridges and a spur at the base. Leaves gray-green, very narrow, 1–2½″ long.

Habitat   Dry fields, roadsides, and waste places.

Range   Throughout much of temperate North America.

Pale Touch-me-not *Impatiens pallida*

Touch-me-nots are related to the Garden Balsam
(*I. balsamina*), which is prized for its colorful flowers.
The name refers to the capsule, which explodes if
touched at maturity and ejects its seeds a distance of
several feet. On humid nights, the leaves droop, and
droplets form on the notches along the edge, ringing the
edge like jewels—thus this plant's other name,
Jewelweed. Spotted Touch-me-not (*I. biflora*) is similar
but has golden-orange flowers, splotched with reddish
brown, and a spur that bends around to the front. Both
bloom from June to October.

Identification	Soft leaves grow on translucent stems; from the tips of branches hang bilateral, red-speckled yellow flowers. Height: 3–6′. Flowers 1½″ long; the lower sepal modified into a broad, petal-like tube with a downward-pointing spur on the tip; 1 upper and 2 lower petals, speckled near opening. Leaves 1–4″ long; broad, pointed, and toothed.
Habitat	Wet woods and meadows; often on wet, shady slopes.
Range	Saskatchewan to Newfoundland, south to North Carolina and upland Georgia, west to Missouri, north to Canada.

88

Common Buttercup *Ranunculus acris*

The buttercup family name—Ranunculaceae—comes from *ranunculus*, meaning "little frog," referring to the wetland habitat of many of the species. There are more than 30 buttercup species in the East. The Common Buttercup, an immigrant from Europe, has an acrid sap that is distasteful to livestock. In general, animals reject buttercups unless no better forage is present; if eaten, the plants cause severe irritation of the digestive tract, and milk produced will have a rancid flavor. Dried buttercups, however, are harmless. Common Buttercup blooms from April to June.

Identification   A hairy plant with shiny, golden-yellow flowers, many stamens and ovaries, 3-lobed and cleft leaves, and bulbous roots. Height: 1–2′. Flower ¾–1″ wide, with 5 broad petals. Basal leaves 1–4″ wide; stalked, cut into 3 lobes and further cleft, the middle lobe stalked, about 1″ long; leaves on the stem smaller and with fewer lobes.

Habitat   Fields, roadsides, lawns, and gardens.

Range   Throughout most of North America.

Canadian Dwarf Cinquefoil *Potentilla canadensis*

Cinquefoils, members of the rose family, resemble buttercups, but have a small, saucerlike receptacle—called a hypanthium—at the base of the flower. Sepals, petals, and stamens attach at the edge of this small "saucer." The name cinquefoil derives from the Latin for "five leaves," in reference to the five segments of the leaf. The genus name comes also from Latin and means "powerful little one"; the various species of *Potentilla* once had many medicinal uses. These plants can hybridize, and identification to species is often difficult. Canadian Dwarf Cinquefoil blooms from March to June.

Identification A single, stalked yellow flower blooms adjacent to a palmately 5-parted leaf; plant is low and finely downy. Height: 2–6″. Flower ½–⅓″ wide, with 5 broad petals. Many stamens and ovaries. Leaf palmately divided into 5 segments; each to 1½″ long, usually more than half as long as wide, and toothed only in the upper half.

Habitat Open areas with dry soil.

Range Ontario to Nova Scotia, south to Georgia, west to Tennessee, Missouri, and Ohio.

92

Yellow Wood Sorrel *Oxalis grandis*

In the fifth century, St. Patrick used a plant with three leaflets to illustrate the doctrine of the Trinity. Today it is still a matter of debate whether this shamrock was a sorrel (*Oxalis*) or a true clover (*Trifolium*). The leaves of this species—also called Sour Grass—can be used sparingly in salads, but large amounts can be slightly toxic. In the East, there are several yellow-flowered *Oxalis* species. Most have somewhat smaller flowers than this plant and a slightly more northerly range, but are otherwise quite similar. Yellow Wood Sorrel blooms from May to October.

Identification   A low, spreading plant with cloverlike leaves and yellow flowers. Height: 8–36″. Flowers ¾–1″ across, with 5 petals and 10 stamens. Leaves have 3 heart-shaped leaflets, ½–¾″ long, that fold in the evening and open in the morning. Stem hairy. Mature capsule explodes when touched.

Habitat   Shady streamsides, woods, and banks.

Range   Pennsylvania to Illinois, and southward.

94

Marsh Marigold *Caltha palustris*

The flowers of this showy spring plant are more like those of the related buttercups than like the Marigold, which is a member of the sunflower family. "Marigold," from "Mary's Gold," in dedication to the Virgin Mary, has been applied over the centuries to a number of deep yellow or golden flowers. Marsh Marigold—also called Cowslip—is toxic, but boiling repeatedly in fresh water removes the toxin and makes the plant edible. It often grows with the deadly Water Hemlock (*Cicuta maculata*), and great care must be taken not to confuse the two. Marsh Marigold blooms from April to June.

Identification A succulent plant with glossy, heart- or kidney-shaped leaves and a thick, hollow, branching stem with bright, shiny yellow flowers. Height: 1–2′. Flowers 1–1½″ wide, with 5–9 petal-like sepals; true petals are lacking. Stamens and pistils are numerous. Leaves 2–7″ wide; basal leaves on long stalks, upper leaves stalkless.

Habitat Swamps, marshes, wet meadows, and streamsides.

Range Across Canada and south through New England to North Carolina, west to Tennessee, Iowa, and Nebraska.

96

Yellow Lady's Slipper *Cypripedium calceolus*

The common name of this flower refers to the yellow pouch formed by the lower petal. Insects are attracted into the pouch; to get out, their route takes them first past the stigma, where they brush off pollen from a previously visited flower, and then under the anther, where they pick up more pollen. There are other eastern species of *Cypripedium* with a white or pink slipper. These orchids are popular wildflowers, and in most areas they have been picked or dug to extinction. Orchids do not grow from seed easily in the wild, and should be left in peace. This species blooms from April to August.

Identification   A leafy stalk bears 1 or 2 fragrant flowers with an inflated yellow pouch formed from the lower petal. Height: 4–28″. Flower lip about 2″ long; 2 spiraled side petals, greenish yellow to brownish purple; sepals 2, lance-shaped. Leaves to 8″; oval or elliptical, with veins.

Habitat   Bogs, swamps, and rich woods.

Range   Throughout the Northern Hemisphere; south in North America to Georgia, Louisiana, Kansas, and New Mexico.

98

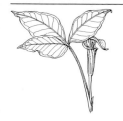

Jack-in-the-pulpit *Arisaema triphyllum*

Jack-in-the-pulpit illustrates the value of using a single scientific name, even if the name seems difficult to learn at first. In the United States alone, there are more than 30 common names for this species, variously referring to the flowers, the root, time of blooming, or that the plant is a kind of an arum lily. Jack-in-the-pulpit's roots are full of fiery-tasting calcium oxalate crystals that can blister sensitive skin. However, if the root is sliced thin and either dried for several months or roasted, the toxin is destroyed and the highly nutritious root becomes palatable. Jack-in-the-pulpit blooms from April to June.

Identification   Large leaves overtop a greenish- or purplish-brown, often streaked, funnel with a "flap" over the top. Height: 1–3′. Flowers tiny; both male and female flowers on the fingerlike spadix in the funnel; funnel (spathe) 3–4″ long. Leaves long-stalked with 3 leaflets; 1 or 2 present. Fruit a cluster of shiny red berries.

Habitat   Damp woods and swamps.

Range   S. Quebec and New Brunswick south in mountains and coastal plain to Florida, Louisiana, and Texas.

100

Squawroot *Conopholis americana*

Squawroot belongs to the broomrape family, a small group of plants that almost completely lack chlorophyll, the green pigment that allows plants to convert the sun's energy into food. Plants in this family are parasites, obtaining all their nutrients through root connections with host plants. In the Old World, some species are agricultural pests, seriously sapping energy from cultivated plants and reducing their yield. Squawroot is usually found in association with oaks and is parasitic upon them. It blooms in May and June.

Identification Entire plant yellowish, fleshy, with thick stems often in clusters; bilateral flowers emerge from scales on the upper part. Height: 3–10″. Flowers ½″ long and 2-lipped; upper lip forming a hood over the 3-lobed lower lip; 4 stamens protrude slightly. Leaves lacking, represented by scales.

Habitat Woods, usually under oaks.

Range Throughout much of the East.

Skunk Cabbage *Symplocarpus foetidus*

Despite its common name, this plant is not a cabbage, but a relative of the florist's Calla Lily. Confusingly, neither one is really a lily; both belong to the arum family, which includes the ornamental *Philodendron*. The large, cabbagey leaves of the Skunk Cabbage may cover large areas of low, moist regions. Its odor, especially when crushed, is garlicky or skunky. This species sprouts early in the spring, and the cellular activity associated with its rapid growth produces heat that melts the snow or ice around the plant. Like Jack-in-the-pulpit, this plant bears tiny flowers on a thumblike spadix, which is surrounded by a modified leaf (called the spathe), mottled with purplish and green. Skunk Cabbage blooms from February to May.

Identification A purplish- and green-mottled spathe encloses a knoblike spadix; large cabbagelike leaves appear later. Height: Spathe 3–6". Leaves 1–2' long, oval, growing directly from a thick, underground stem.

Habitat Open swamps and marshes, stream banks, wet woods.

Range Much of S. Canada south to Iowa and upland Georgia.

104

Northern Pitcher Plant *Sarracenia purpurea*

These bizarre plants belong to a tiny family of 17 species. Their peculiar leaves and carnivorous habit make them a desirable curiosity, and many have disappeared from the wild; the rarest are protected by law. The leaves of these plants collect rainwater; insects, attracted by the reddish lip and the odor, enter the leaf. The slippery sides have downcurved hairs that make escape difficult. Finally the insect falls, drowns, and is digested by bacterial action and enzymes secreted by the plant. Northern Pitcher Plant blooms from May to August.

Identification A solitary, purplish-red flower on a leafless stalk blooms above a rosette of bronzy reddish-green leaves, which are curled and inflated. Height: 8–24″. Flowers 2″ wide, with 5 petals, numerous stamens, and an umbrellalike style. Leaves 4–12″ long, the flaring lip covered with stiff hairs.

Habitat Sphagnum bogs.

Range Saskatchewan to Labrador and Nova Scotia, south through New England to Florida, west to Texas, north to Minnesota.

106

Wild Columbine *Aquilegia canadensis*

This lovely wild plant is popular in the garden, either unchanged or hybridized into large and colorful forms. It is related to the buttercups, but its flowers are quite different: The petals have scooplike ends extending into nectar-filled spurs that reward the hungry hummingbird. Pollination results as the hovering bird's belly rubs against the anthers and the stigma. Bumblebees often pierce the spur and steal nectar without pollinating the flower. Wild Columbine blooms from April to July.

Identification   A nodding red and yellow flower; upward-directed spurs from the petals alternate with spreading red sepals; numerous yellow stamens hang below the petals. Height: 1–2'. Flowers 1–2" long; 5 petals, each with a yellow "sugar scoop" opening to the hollow red spur; 5 broad red sepals taper to fine points. Leaves many times divided into fan-shaped, lobed leaflets, ½–1¼" long.

Habitat   Rocky, wooded, or open slopes.

Range   Ontario to Quebec, south throughout New England to Georgia, west to central Texas, Tennessee, and Wisconsin.

108

Turk's-cap Lily *Lilium superbum*

This is the largest and the showiest of the native lilies: As many as 40 flowers have been recorded on a single plant. The bulbs of these and their seven or eight eastern relatives were dug by Native Americans for food. These lilies are still taken and used as garden plants, a practice that has made them very rare in many areas—but given a chance, they soon return in large numbers. Turk's-cap Lily gets its name from the shape of the flower. The similar Carolina Lily (*L. michauxii*) lacks this species' greenish star pattern in the center. Turk's-cap Lily blooms from July to September.

Identification Nodding orange flowers, spotted with reddish brown, have strongly recurved petals and sepals; a green streak at the base of each of these forms a star in the center of the flower. Height: 3–7′. Flowers 2½″ long; sepals and petals alike, brightly colored; stamens conspicuous. Leaves lance-shaped, 2–6″ long; usually in rings on the stem.

Habitat Wet meadows, swamps, and woods.

Range S. New Hampshire, Massachusetts, and New York south to Georgia and Alabama.

110

Flame Azalea *Rhododendron calendulaceum*

This flamboyant deciduous shrub, with flowers ranging from yellow through orange to scarlet, forms striking displays on high mountain openings. Botanists now tend to include all azaleas in the genus *Rhododendron*, a group of about 200 species, although as a common name rhododendron is applied mostly to evergreen shrubs. The azaleas and rhododendrons are found primarily in the East, and also in eastern Asia; hybrids between species from home and afar have produced some of our most spectacular ornamentals. As members of the heath family, most are lovers of acid soil. Flame Azalea blooms in May and June.

Identification   A deciduous shrub with clusters of flaring orange, scarlet, or yellow flowers. Height: 3–15′. Flowers 1½–2″ wide; the 5 petal lobes joined into a tubular base, forming a star; exceeded by the 5 slender stamens and style. Leaves 2–4″ long; oval and pointed at tip.

Habitat   Dry, open woods and mountain balds.

Range   SW. Pennsylvania through the mountains to Georgia and Alabama, west to West Virginia and SE. Ohio.

112

Butterfly Weed *Asclepias tuberosa*

The warm hues of yellow, red, and orange, and its attractiveness to butterflies, make this species a popular garden plant. It is a "milkweed" (*Asclepias*), but does not have milky sap. Like the others in the genus, Butterfly Weed has a complicated flower to aid a very precise and improbable pollination mechanism—a packet of pollen must be precisely inserted into a receiving slit by an insect. This arrangement explains why there are so few pods on a milkweed, but when a pod is formed, the hundreds of seeds produced compensate for the rarity of the event. This plant blooms from June to September.

Identification   Rounded clusters of bright yellow to red-orange flowers crown the top of a leafy stem. Height: 1–2½'. Flowers about ⅜" wide, with 5 curved-back petals attached to a central crown made of 5 scooplike hoods. Flower stalks all attach to the same point. Leaves narrow, alternate on the stem; 2–6" long. Pod spindle-shaped, hairy, erect.

Habitat   Dry, open roadsides, hillsides, and fields.

Range   Ontario to Newfoundland and New England, south to Arizona, Colorado, and Florida.

Indian Paintbrush *Castilleja coccinea*

Indian Paintbrush is a conspicuous but distant relative of the snapdragon. One of the few eastern representatives of a huge western genus, it is simultaneously a bit of a sham and a minor thief. The brilliant red comes not from the petals, but from the coloration of the calyx and the upper leaflike bracts among the flowers; the rest of the flower is small and protrudes as a beak. These plants may have perfectly good roots, but they often attach to the roots of other plants and steal nutrients. Indian Paintbrush blooms from May to July.

Identification   Ragged, paintbrushlike cluster of fan-shaped, scarlet-tipped bracts nearly hides beaklike flowers at the top of a leafy stem. Height: 1–2′. Flower 1″ wide; tubular beak with a green bump, or lip, midway; calyx deeply notched above and below, but not on sides. Bracts scarlet in the outer half, 3-lobed. Leaves narrow, 1–3″ long at the base, sometimes cleft.

Habitat   Meadows, prairies, and damp, sandy soil.

Range   S. Manitoba to S. New Hampshire, south to N. Florida, west to Louisiana and Oklahoma.

116

Fire Pink *Silene virginica*

Fire Pink resembles some of the simple relatives of the many-petaled carnations, or "pinks." The fire-engine red flower suggests that hummingbirds may be important pollinators. The sticky hairs on the plant provide another common name for the genus, Catchfly—small insects landing on the plant remain stuck there. There are two other red-flowered species in the East: Royal Catchfly (*S. regia*) has no well-defined notch at the ends of the petals; Roundleaf Catchfly (*S. rotundifolia*) has five to eight pairs of roundish leaves. Fire Pink blooms from April to June.

Identification   Loose clusters of bright red flowers bloom on long stalks at the tops of slender, sticky stems with paired leaves. Height: 6–24″. Flowers 1½″ wide, with 5 narrow, often deeply cleft petals; calyx tubular. Leaves to 6″ long, paired; 2–4 pairs present.

Habitat   Open woods, thickets, and rocky or sandy slopes.

Range   S. Ontario south to Georgia, west to Arkansas and Oklahoma, north to Minnesota.

Cardinal Flower *Lobelia cardinalis*

The common name of this handsome plant alludes to the bright red robes worn by Roman Catholic cardinals. Its color, unusual in a genus of ordinarily blue or blue-violet flowers, attracts hummingbirds, which can extract nectar from the long, tubular base. The anthers, which are joined into a tube, place pollen on the closed stigma as it pushes through. Later, after most of the pollen has been carried to other flowers by birds or insects, the stigma opens and becomes receptive to pollen. The Cardinal Flower is highly toxic, but livestock avoid it because of its taste. It blooms from July to September.

Identification   Loose spires of bilateral, brilliant red flowers atop an erect stalk. Height: 2–6'. Flowers 1½" long, with 2 lobes on the upper lip, and 3 on the lower, the tube slit along the sides; 5 stamens, united by anthers to form a tube. Leaves lance-shaped, toothed, to 6" long.

Habitat   Damp places, along streams, and on hillside seeps.

Range   S. Ontario to New Brunswick, south to Florida, west to Texas, north to Minnesota; also SW. United States and south into Mexico.

Trumpet Honeysuckle *Lonicera sempervirens*

The honeysuckles are popular garden plants, as much for their sweet, copious nectar and sweet scent as for their appearance. One of the cultivated species, Japanese Honeysuckle (*L. japonica*), introduced from eastern Asia, has left the gardens and become a serious woodland weed, smothering native vegetation. In that twining species, the white to pale apricot flowers grow in pairs at the end of a stalk that originates in the angle of the leaf and stem. Trumpet Honeysuckle is easily distinguished from the other species by its large, bright, barely two-lipped flower. It blooms from April to August.

Identification A vine with showy, trumpet-shaped flowers, red or deep yellow outside, yellow inside, in 2 groups of 3; flowers form 1 or more rings of 6 flowers on the stem. Height: A climbing vine. Flowers 1–2″ long, with 5 barely flared petal lobes. Leaves deep green, 1½–3″ long; oblong and paired on the stem, with uppermost pair joined at base.

Habitat Woods and thickets.

Range Massachusetts and New York south to Florida, west to Texas, Ohio, Iowa, and Nebraska; escaped elsewhere.

122

Scarlet Pimpernel *Anagallis arvensis*

This delicate weed of flower beds and open places is a relative of cyclamen and primrose. The flowers deserve a close look with a lens, for the intricate pattern of violet in the center contrasts handsomely with the salmon. This species is also called the Poorman's Weatherglass, for the flowers close in cloudy weather. The plant is said to be poisonous, and the leaves may cause dermatitis in certain sensitive people. This plant was once used to alleviate melancholy, perhaps because its cheery flowers, blooming from June to August, appear after cloudy times.

Identification A sprawling herb with paired leaves, 4-sided stems, and flat pinkish-orange (rarely blue or white) blossoms on threadlike stalks. Height: 4–12″. Flowers ⅙″ wide, with 5 petal lobes fringed with minute teeth. Stamens have bearded filaments. Leaves paired, ¼–1¼″ long; broad, without stalks. Fruit a round capsule, opening by a lid that pops off.

Habitat Loose soil in gardens, waste places, and roadsides.

Range Throughout temperate North America.

124

Virginia Meadow Beauty *Rhexia virginica*

Virginia Meadow Beauty is one of the few temperate representatives of a fairly large tropical family comprised mostly of trees and shrubs. In the East, there are perhaps ten species of *Rhexia*, whose urn-shaped fruit Thoreau likened to a little cream pitcher. The seeds are peculiar in that they are coiled and resemble tiny snail shells. The odd stamens, with their downcurved anthers, help to identify this and several other species in the genus. Virginia Meadow Beauty blooms from July to September.

Identification Several pink flowers, with conspicuous, curved, yellow anthers, form terminal clusters on a sturdy, 4-sided, slightly winged stem. Height: 1–2′. Flowers 1–1½″ across, with 4 broad petals; stamens have large curved anthers, with a knob at the base and terminal pores. Leaves ¾–2½″ long; paired, broadly lance-shaped or broader, with 3–5 prominent veins.

Habitat Wet sands and peat bogs.

Range Nova Scotia to Ontario, south to Florida, west to Mississippi, Tennessee, and Missouri.

126

Bouncing Bet *Saponaria officinalis*

Nearly 2000 years ago, the Greek physician Dioscorides recorded the usefulness of this plant; added to water, its crushed leaves produce a lather. Later, colonial housewives sometimes used this lather as an alternative to lye soap; for this reason, the plant is also called Soapwort. The plant is toxic but distasteful, and therefore not a problem for livestock. Bouncing Bet is an old nickname for a washerwoman. This species blooms from July to September.

Identification Leafy, sparingly branched plant, swollen where the paired leaves join the stem, with the fragrant white or pinkish flowers in a terminal cluster. Height: 1–3'. Flowers about 1" wide; 5 delicate petals scalloped on the end and with small appendages at the opening of the flower. Leaves 2–3" long, paired on the stem; oval, with 3–5 conspicuous veins.

Habitat Roadsides and other disturbed areas.

Range Nearly throughout temperate North America.

Nodding Wild Onion *Allium cernuum*

This is the only onion in the East whose stalk bends like a shepherd's crook under the weight of the nodding flower cluster. The bulbs of all *Allium* species are edible, although some have an extremely potent and unpleasing flavor. In the early days of exploration of the West, more than one party was saved from scurvy by Native Americans, who alerted the explorers to the curative properties of wild onions. Old World species have produced the many varieties of cultivated onions, garlic, chives, leeks, and scallions. Nodding Wild Onion blooms from July to August.

Identification   Flowers bell-shaped, rose, pink, or white, and in a nodding cluster atop a leafless stem. Height: 8–24″. Flowers ¼″ long, with 3 petals and 3 petal-like sepals. Leaves narrow and flat; 4–16″ long.

Habitat   Open woods and rocky soil.

Range   New York to Minnesota, south to Virginia, Kentucky, and Missouri; in the mountains to Georgia and Alabama; also in the West.

Twinflower *Linnaea borealis*

This delicate plant, the only species in its genus, occurs in cool woods and bogs almost throughout the Northern Hemisphere. It seems strange that Twinflower should be a relative of the honeysuckle or elderberry, but the technical aspects of the plant assure us that it is. The scientific genus name honors Carolus Linnaeus, the famed 18th-century Swedish botanist who devised the first consistent method of naming plants—the method that we use today. The "father of modern botany" was fond of the Twinflower, and the species was named for him at his own suggestion. Twinflower blooms from June to August, and its scent is said to be strongest at night.

Identification   A trailing, evergreen plant with upright branches ending in paired, nodding flowers, which are slender and bell-shaped. Height: 3–6″. Flowers about ½″ long; whitish near the 5 lobes; pinkish on the tube; hairy inside. Leaves about ½″ long, oval; toothed and opposite.

Habitat   Cool woods and bogs.

Range   Alaska to Greenland, south to South Dakota, Indiana, Ohio, West Virginia, and Maryland.

132

Purple Loosestrife *Lythrum salicaria*

Purple Loosestrife was probably introduced to the North American continent from Europe as an ornamental. It is truly spectacular when in bloom; however, it is very aggressive and tends to crowd out valuable native aquatics. Purple Loosestrife is not at all closely related to the loosestrifes (*Lysimachia*) of the primrose family— a fact that shows the value of scientific names. This species blooms from June to September.

Identification An erect stem with a spike of purple-pink flowers and unstalked leaves paired or in rings along the stem. Height: 2–5′. Flowers ½–¾″ wide, with 4–6 crinkled petals and twice as many stamens; stamen and pistil lengths vary; sepals form a tube to which petals and stamens attach. Leaves very narrow to lance-shaped, 1½–4″ long.

Habitat Wet meadows, floodplains, marshes, and roadside ditches.

Range E. Canada south to Virginia and Missouri; sporadic in the West.

Purple Prairie Clover *Petalostemum purpureum*

The colorful heads of Prairie Clover, the divided leaves, and its membership in the pea family all help to provide the common name for this species. However, the true clovers, so important for forage and lawns, belong to the genus *Trifolium*. An excellent range species with high protein content, Purple Prairie Clover tends to decrease in abundance where grazing is heavy. The similar White Prairie Clover (*P. candidum*) occurs in the Midwest and on the Great Plains. Purple Prairie Clover blooms from June to September.

Identification Tiny rose-purple flowers in cylindrical headlike masses at the ends of upright, wiry stems. Height: 1–3′. Flowers about ⅙″ long, in heads to 2″ long; upper petal broad and heart-shaped, the 4 lower petals narrower; stamens 5; calyx has small, dark gland dots. Leaves pinnately divided into 3–7 (usually 5) narrow segments, ½–¾″ long; with small, dark gland dots.

Habitat Prairies, dry hills, and roadsides.

Range Indiana and W. Tennessee southwest to Arkansas, Texas, New Mexico, and north to Canadian Great Plains.

136

Spotted Joe-Pye Weed *Eupatorium maculatum*

According to folklore, Joe Pye was a Native American living in New England in the late 1700's who used this plant and its relatives to cure fevers. Early American colonists used it to treat a variety of ailments and gave it the names Ague Weed, Indian Sage, Kidney-root, and Gravel-root. It is one of several similar species in the East: Sweet Joe-Pye Weed (*E. purpureum*) has a dome-shaped cluster of dull pink flower heads, a greenish stem, and leaves that smell like vanilla when crushed; Hollow Joe-Pye Weed (*E. fistulosum*) has a hollow stem; and *E. dubium* is smaller with egg-shaped, pointed leaves. Spotted Joe-Pye Weed blooms from July to September.

Identification Sturdy purple or purple-spotted stem, hairy above, bears a cluster of pinkish-purplish, flat-topped flowers with fuzzy heads. Height: 2–6′. Flower heads ⅓″ wide, in clusters 4–5½″ wide. Leaves lance-shaped, coarsely toothed; 2½–8″ long, in rings of 3–5.

Habitat Damp meadows, thickets, and shores.

Range Across S. Canada and N. United States; south in mountainous areas to North Carolina.

138

Rough Blazing Star *Liatris aspera*

The blazing stars (*Liatris* spp.) provide late-season color throughout the East and across the Great Plains to the eastern flank of the Rockies. Their bright pink spires of ragged heads give rise to another descriptive common name for the group, gay-feathers. These flowers are a genus of about 40 species in the sunflower family; the group is made complex by its numbers and hybridization. Rough Blazing Star, so named because of its rough hairs, blooms from August to October.

Identification   Rounded lavender-pink flower heads in a loose, spikelike cluster; stiff, erect stems are covered with rough, grayish hairs. Height: 1–4′. Flower heads about ½″ long, broadly cup-shaped, with or without individual stalks; flower heads have broadly rounded, flaring bracts, with pinkish, translucent, often fringed, margins. Leaves rough; lance-shaped or narrower; lower leaves 4–12″ long, upper ones progressively smaller.

Habitat   In sandy soil on plains and in open woods.

Range   Manitoba and Ontario south to South Carolina, west to Texas, and north to North Dakota.

140

Bull Thistle *Cirsium vulgare*

This stout weed of pastures is probably one of the world's most unloved plants. Its thick stem, formidable spines, and tough root make it difficult to eradicate; what is more, the "thistledown"—feathery bristles atop the seedlike fruit—carries seeds long distances and ensures that new plants will soon establish themselves. Despite its unpopularity, this member of the sunflower family produces fine honey. Bull Thistle, introduced from Europe, can be distinguished from the numerous other purple-headed species by the large "wings" running down the stem. It blooms from June to September.

Identification   Stout plants with spiny leaves and a spiny, winged stem; rose-purple flower heads enclosed in a spiny-bracted base. Height: 2–6'. Flower heads 1½–2" wide. Leaves 3–6" long, coarsely pinnately lobed, very spiny. Fruit bears fine bristles with hundreds of short, minute branches, resembling miniature plumes.

Habitat   Roadsides, pastures, and waste places.

Range   Throughout most of temperate North America.

Wild Bergamot *Monarda fistulosa*

This handsome member of the mint family shows how misleading common names can be: Bergamot is an unrelated citrus grown for aromatic oils; Wild Bergamot has a somewhat similar odor. A pleasant mint tea, said to have had its greatest popularity after the Boston Tea Party, can be made from Wild Bergamot. The related scarlet-flowered Oswego Tea or Bee Balm (*M. didyma*), is found throughout the East. Both species, but especially Wild Bergamot, are cultivated. Wild Bergamot blooms from June to September.

Identification   A dense, rounded cluster of deep lavender, strongly bilateral tubular flowers blooms at the top of a 4-sided stem. Height: 2–4'. Flowers about 1" long, with hairy, 2-lobed upper lip and broader, 3-lobed lower lip; 2 stamens project from the flower opening. Leaves paired on the stem, lance-shaped; 2–4" long, with coarse teeth.

Habitat   Dry fields, thickets, and woodland borders; usually common in calcareous (limey) soils.

Range   Manitoba and Quebec south to E. Texas, Louisiana, Maryland, and upland Georgia and Alabama.

144

Chicory *Cichorium intybus*

According to legend, Chicory is Florilor, a gentle lady who was transformed into a flower when she rejected the advances of the sun god. In her altered form she mocks him, watching until noon, then closing her flowers and ignoring his presence. For centuries Chicory has been prized as a love potion, the seeds secretly administered by a suitor to secure the affection of his lady. The young leaves are edible, rather like those of the related Endive (*C. endivia*). The plant has been used to prevent scurvy, as a mild sedative, and for skin irritations. Today, the root is cultivated and roasted as a coffee substitute or extender. Chicory blooms from June to October.

Identification   Stiff, wiry stems with few leaves bear showy, windmill like flower heads, which are clear blue. Height: 1–5′. Heads to 1½″ wide, with numerous broad, square-tipped, fringed rays; dark blue anthers surround threadlike, 2-part style. Leaves 3–6″ long; largest at the base and coarsely toothed on edges.

Habitat   Fields, roadsides, and waste places.

Range   Throughout most of temperate North America.

146

Wild Mint *Mentha arvensis*

Species of mint are common wildflowers in damp places, but all except this one are European imports—most were brought with the colonists as culinary or medicinal herbs. Wild Mint can be distinguished from them all by the clusters of flowers at the bases of leaves and by the calyx, which is hairy all over. This species contains essential oils that may be distilled to make peppermint or spearmint flavors; its distinctive aroma is characteristic of most members of the family. Wild Mint blooms from July to September.

Identification Plant with a strong, minty odor, bearing tiny, bell-shaped, pale lilac or white flower clusters in circles around the stem; stem finely hairy on the angles where the paired leaves arise. Height: 6–24". Flowers about ¼" long, with 4 petal lobes and 4 stamens. Leaves to 2" long; lance-shaped or broader.

Habitat Damp and wet places with plenty of sunlight.

Range Throughout the East; common in much of temperate North America.

148

Stiff Aster *Aster linariifolius*

Species of *Aster* are legion; in the Northeast alone, there are more than 60, and even botanists find that accurate identification can be difficult. Asters also have look-alikes in the genus *Machaeranthera*, some of which can be distinguished only by close examination. All asters are spectacular wildflowers, adding splashes of pale lavender or vibrant purple to open patches in the woods or to entire fields. Some have given rise to popular late-season ornamentals known as "Michaelmas Daisies." The Stiff Aster, also called Bristly Aster, blooms from August to October.

Identification   Numerous short, stiff, leafy stems form a mound of pale lavender to deep pink daisylike flowers. Height: 8–18". Flower heads to 1" wide, with narrow pale lavender to bright pink rays surrounding a yellow center. Leaves very narrow, dark green; ½–1¼" long. Fruit seedlike, with many soft, slender, tawny bristles at the top.

Habitat   Dry clearings and open banks.

Range   E. Canada and New England to NW. Florida, west to Louisiana and E. Texas, north to Minnesota.

150

Rugosa Rose *Rosa rugosa*

Blooming wild on the beaches and among the dunes of the Northeast, this lovely flower is a cheerful sight. According to one Greek legend, it was Chloris, goddess of flowers, who created this delight when she granted to a lovely nymph life as a flower. To the new flower, Aphrodite gave beauty; the three Graces bestowed brilliance, joy, and charm; and Bacchus, master of the revels, gave nectar and fragrance. Chloris presented her creation to Eros, god of love, and the red rose became the symbol of love and desire. In North America, there are many wild roses, some similar to this fragrant species, which blooms from June to September.

Identification   Large rose-lavender flowers (rarely white) borne on very spiny stems with finely corrugated leaves. Height: 4–6'. Flowers 2–3″ wide, with 5 broad petals and numerous bright yellow stamens. Leaves 3–6″ long, pinnately divided into oval, toothed, wrinkled leaflets.

Habitat   Seashore thickets and sand dunes.

Range   Quebec to Nova Scotia and New England, west to Illinois, Wisconsin, and Minnesota.

Common Morning Glory *Ipomoea purpurea*

Most species of *Ipomoea* are twining plants—the genus name comes from a combination of two Greek words meaning "worm" and "bindweed." Many are very popular cultivated plants, blooming in the morning, the flower twisting closed by the heat of midday. The Common Morning Glory is a native of tropical America and has escaped from cultivation in this country. Ivy-leaved Morning Glory (*I. hederacea*) has three-lobed leaves and sepals that taper to very slender points. Although pretty, it has become a serious agricultural weed in the South. The Sweet Potato (*I. batatas*), also from tropical America, is in the same genus. Common Morning Glory blooms from July to October.

Identification A twining vine with showy, funnel-shaped flowers of purple, pink, blue, or white; with hairy stems and heart-shaped leaves. Height: Climbing to 10′. Flowers 2–3″ long, with pointed, hairy sepals. Leaves 2–5″ long.

Habitat Cultivated fields, roadsides, old lots, and waste places.

Range Throughout much of temperate North America.

154

Fringed Polygala *Polygala paucifolia*

The delightful flower of this species might fancifully be likened to the head of a miniature pink rabbit chewing a pom-pom. Sometimes called Gaywings, it belongs to a genus generally known as "milkworts," because it was thought that some species, if eaten by nursing mothers or fed to cows, would increase the flow of milk. Fringed Polygala, with the largest flowers of all eastern *Polygala* species, blooms in May and June.

Identification	A low plant, growing from prostrate underground stems and rootstocks, with 1–4 strongly bilateral, fringed pink flowers at the top of the stem. Height: 3–7″. Flowers ¾″ long; 2 bright pink lateral sepals (forming the "rabbit's ears"); 3 united petals forming a tube; lowest petal ending in a delicate, finely fringed yellow or pink crest (the "pom-pom"). Leaves oval, ¾–1½″ long; topmost leaves crowded, lower ones small and bractlike.
Habitat	Rich, moist woods.
Range	Manitoba to New Brunswick, south through New England, inland to Virginia and the mountains of Georgia, west to Tennessee, N. Illinois, and Minnesota.

Monkeyflower *Mimulus ringens*

Monkeyflowers are in the snapdragon family, and their bilateral flowers attest to the relationship. The genus is widespread, but is especially well developed in the West. In the East, the only other blue-flowered species is Sharp-winged Monkeyflower (*M. alatus*), which has stalked leaves and a winged stem. Among the three yellow-flowered species, the smooth, sprawling Yellow Monkeyflower (*M. glabratus*), a native species, and the moist-hairy Muskflower (*M. moschatus*), which is escaped from cultivation, are common in wet places. "Monkeyflower" refers to the impish, facelike look of the flowers. Monkeyflower blooms from June to September.

Identification Bilateral, 2-lipped blue-purple flowers bloom at the bases of paired leaves that clasp the 4-sided stem. Height: 1–3′. Flowers about 1″ long; upper lip erect and 2-lobed, the lower lip bent down, 3-lobed, with a yellow blotch near the opening. Leaves 2–4″; lance-shaped, stalkless.

Habitat Wet meadows and banks of streams.

Range Saskatchewan to Nova Scotia, south to Georgia, west to Alabama, Louisiana, and NE. Texas.

158

Blue Flag *Iris versicolor*

The genus name *Iris* honors a member of Juno's court, the goddess of the rainbow, who so impressed Juno with her purity that she was commemorated with a flower that bloomed in all the colors of her robe. Iris flowers have a unique structure. In the terminology of horticulture, the declined petal-like sepals form the "falls," and the more erect petals are the "standards." The underground stem, or rhizome, of this species is extremely poisonous, although Native Americans and colonists dried it for use as a cathartic. There are several irises in the East; this one blooms from May to August.

Identification Several violet-blue flowers with attractively veined and yellow-based sepals on a sturdy stalk; tall, swordlike leaves arise from the base. Height: 2–3'. Flowers 2½–4" across; sepals 3, not bearded along the middle; petals 3, narrower, erect. Leaves 8–32" long, ½–1" wide. Fruit a bluntly 3-lobed capsule.

Habitat Swamps, marshes, and freshwater shores.

Range Manitoba to Nova Scotia, south through New England to Virginia, west to W. Pennsylvania, Ohio, and Minnesota.

Wild Lupine *Lupinus perennis*

The windmill-like leaves and the spires of pealike flowers, which ally this plant with the giant garden lupine, may form extensive patches of soft blue. The common and genus names come from the Latin *lupus,* for "wolf," from the belief that lupines "wolf" nutrients from the soil. To the contrary, many species prefer poor earth, and from an association with bacteria living in their roots, add nitrogen—a precious fertilizer for other species—to the soil. Texas Bluebonnet (*L. subcarnosus*), with its side petals, or wings, puffed out like little cheeks, is the state flower of Texas. Wild Lupine blooms from April to July.

Identification	Windmill like leaves grow beneath spires of blue pealike flowers. Height: 8–24″. Flowers to ⅔″ long; upper petal ("banner") with a pale patch in the center. Leaves palmately compound into 7–11 lance-shaped leaflets, each to 2″ long.
Habitat	Dry, open woods and fields.
Range	Maine to Florida, west to Louisiana and Minnesota.

162

Large Purple Fringed Orchid *Habenaria fimbriata*

The genus name comes from the Latin *habena* ("rein"), referring to the long, reinlike spur in some species; these flowers are often called the "rein orchids." When an insect approaches to feed on nectar in the spur, the pollen sac (pollinium) adheres to it; when the insect backs out, it pulls the pollinium free and carries it to the next flower. The precise position of the pollinium on the insect ensures that it pollinates the next flower when it enters. The Small Purple Fringed Orchid (*H. psycodes*) has smaller flowers; some experts believe the two are the same species. Both bloom from June to August.

Identification   Many deeply fringed, fragrant lavender flowers in a long cluster on a leafy stem. Height: 2–4′. Flower 1″ long; lower lip has 3 fan-shaped fringed lobes and a backward-pointing spur; the upper sepal and 2 lateral petals are erect, lateral sepals broader and spreading. Basal leaves lance-shaped or broader, to 8″; stem leaves smaller.

Habitat   Cool moist woods, wet meadows, and swamp margins.

Range   Ontario to Newfoundland, south to Maryland and West Virginia; in mountains to North Carolina and Tennessee.

164

Pickerelweed *Pontederia cordata*

Pickerelweed belongs to a small, mostly tropical family of aquatic plants. It is typically found in shallow, quiet water. The inside of the leafstalk is composed of large, loosely packed cells with large air spaces between. This structure allows oxygen to reach the submerged parts of the plant and gives maximum support for a minimum commitment of tissue—a nice feat of natural engineering. The young leafstalks can be cooked as greens, and the seeds eaten like nuts. Pickerelweed blooms from June to November.

Identification An aquatic herb with blue flower spikes and heart-shaped leaves extending above the water. Height: 1–2′ above the water. Flowers ⅛″ long; funnel-shaped, with a 3-lobed upper lip marked with 2 yellow spots in the middle, and 3 separate lower parts. Leaves 4–10″ long, heart-shaped, on long stalks.

Habitat Freshwater marshes, ponds, lakes, and streams.

Range Ontario to Nova Scotia and New England, south to N. Florida, west to Missouri and Oklahoma, north to Minnesota.

166

Viper's Bugloss *Echium vulgare*

This Mediterranean species arrived in North America by the 1680's, possibly in hay used to pack breakables in transit. Once here, it spread inexorably westward, for it is fully at home almost anywhere that land is disturbed. Annoyed by this beautiful pest, farmers have given it less complimentary names, including Blue Devil and Blueweed. Each of four seedlike fruit segments has the shape of a viper's head; "bugloss" comes from the Greek for "ox tongue," in reference to the broad, rough leaves. Viper's Bugloss blooms from June to October.

Identification   Hairy plant with broadly flared blue flowers, each with protruding red stamens, in branches of coiled clusters arranged on a long central stalk. Height: 1 2½'. Flowers about ¾" long; tubular at the base, broadly flared, with 5 petal lobes; pink at first, maturing to blue, with 5 protruding stamens. Leaves rough-hairy and broadly lance-shaped; 2–6" long.

Habitat   Fields, roadsides, and waste places.

Range   Throughout the Northeast, but not south of South Carolina or Tennessee.

168

Virginia Bluebells *Mertensia virginica*

These soft plants, growing in masses, make a spectacular show. They are smooth, unlike many of the harshly hairy members of the borago family, but like them have flowers that bloom from an uncoiling cluster. Sometimes called Virginia Cowslip, this plant is related to other cowslips—apparently plants of cow pastures. The hanging blue flowers, tubular but with a flared end, are distinctive. Two eastern relatives are Sea Lungwort (*M. maritima*), from the New England coast, with flowers only about ⅓″ long, and Tall Lungwort (*M. paniculata*), which has sparsely hairy leaves. Virginia Bluebells blooms from March to June.

Identification Erect plant with smooth gray-green foliage and nodding clusters of pink buds that open into trumpet-shaped, light blue flowers. Height: 8–24″. Flowers ¾–1″ long; tubular, but 5-lobed and flared at the end. Basal leaves oval, pointed, 2–8″ long; those on the stem smaller.

Habitat Moist woods; rarely in meadows.

Range S. Ontario to W. New York, south to E. Kansas, Arkansas, Alabama, and N. North Carolina.

170

Harebell *Campanula rotundifolia*

The genus name for this delightful little wildflower means "little bell," and is perfectly descriptive. Some species of *Campanula*, such as Canterbury Bells and various bellflowers, are popular in gardens, providing a handsome blue accent. The name Harebell may allude to an association with witches, who were believed able to transform themselves into hares—portents of bad luck when they crossed a person's path. This species is also called Bluebell; in Scotland, another old name for it was Witches' Thimble. It blooms from June to September.

Identification   Bell-shaped, blue-violet flowers hang from threadlike stalks at the top of slender stems. Height: 4–40″. Flowers ½–1″ long, with 5 bluntly pointed petal lobes that gently curve outward; style about as long as petals, not protruding. Leaves near base and on stem very narrow, and ½–3″ long; basal leaves, when present, broadly oval.

Habitat   Rocky banks and slopes, meadows, and shores.

Range   N. Canada through the Northeast and the Midwest; south in the mountains of the West to Mexico.

Bittersweet Nightshade *Solanum dulcamara*

Some nightshades are edible, but others are toxic—even deadly. The attractive red berries of this species, when eaten in quantity, are poisonous. Common Nightshade (*S. americanum*), a low plant with white flowers, has black berries that are toxic at first, but their toxicity decreases as they ripen. The Potato (*S. tuberosum*) is an important food crop worldwide, yet its green parts are toxic. The huge purple-black berry of *S. melongena* is familiar to us as the Eggplant. Bittersweet Nightshade (also called Climbing Nightshade) blooms from May to September.

Identification   A climbing plant bearing loose, flattish clusters of drooping blue or violet star-shaped flowers with a yellow "beak" of anthers in the center. Height: Climbing to 8'. Flower about ½" wide; 5 joined petals form the points of the star and are often bent back. Leaves to 3½" long, broad, often with a pair of lobes at the base. Fruit a shiny green berry that becomes red at maturity.

Habitat   Thickets and clearings.

Range   Throughout much of temperate North America.

174

Common Blue Violet *Viola papilionacea*

The popularity of this jaunty violet is far-reaching: a symbol of modesty and simplicity, the emblem of French Bonapartists, the quintessential flower of March, and the state flower of Illinois, New Jersey, Rhode Island, and Wisconsin. The leaves are nutritious and can be used in salads and cooked as greens; the flowers may be used in candies and jellies. In addition to the eye-catching flowers, there are flowers near the ground that do not open, but produce abundant seed. Violets hybridize, making identification to species difficult. This flower, also called Meadow Violet, blooms from March to June.

Identification | A smooth low plant with bilateral flowers blue to white, or white with purple veins; heart-shaped leaves appear on separate stalks. Height: 3–8″. Flowers ½–¾″ wide; the lowest of 5 petals longer and spurred, the lateral 2 bearded. Leaves to 5″ long, with scalloped margins.

Habitat | Damp woods, moist meadows, and roadsides.

Range | Throughout the East.

176

True Forget-me-not *Myosotis scorpioides*

This species is a member of the forget-me-not family, recognizable by the curled flower cluster and the four seedlike nutlets that develop from the ovary. One name for the plant is Scorpion Weed, alluding to the coiled flower cluster. Another, Mouse-ear, a translation of the genus name, refers to the small, earlike leaves. Legends surrounding the origin of "forget-me-not" are many; most involve a medieval suitor reaching too far over a cliff to obtain a delicate blue flower for his lover—and crying out, "Forget me not!" while falling to his death. This species blooms from May to October.

Identification   Perennial plant with small blue flowers with yellow "eyes" around the tube, at the tops of coils on divergent branches. Height: 6–24″. Flowers ¼″ wide; calyx hairs lie flat, not hooked or spreading. Leaves 1–2″ long; oblong, blunt, and hairy; mostly stalkless.

Habitat   Stream borders and wet places.

Range   Nearly throughout the East, but more common in the North; also westward.

178

Bluets *Houstonia caerulea*

Bluets belong to a North American genus of striking, delicate, often tufted plants forming bright patches of pale blue or pale blue-violet. There are a number of species of bluets, all recognizable by their low habit, the tubular flowers that flare into four petal lobes, and the opposite leaves on the stem. Several species of bluets, including this one, are cultivated for their showy flowers. Bluets bloom from April to June.

Identification A low plant with slender, erect stems bearing pale blue, pale lavender, or white flowers with a yellow "eye" in the center. Height: 3–6″. Flower about ½″ wide; 4 petal lobes at right angles to the narrow tube. Lower leaves ¼–½″ long; oblong, on stalks nearly as long; upper leaves stalkless. Fruit flattish, with 2 lobes, about ⅙″ wide.

Habitat Grassy slopes and fields, thickets, and lawns with acid soils.

Range Ontario to Novia Scotia, south to Georiga, west to Alabama, north to Wisconsin.

Wild Blue Phlox *Phlox divaricata*

Phloxes are popular wildflowers, with white, pink, or blue-purple blossoms that nearly cover the entire plant. A number of species are grown in gardens. This plant, sometimes called Wild Sweet William, has the unique flower structure that characterizes the phlox family. Plants of Wild Blue Phlox in the eastern part of the range have a notch in the petals; those in the western portion do not. There are a number of species in the East, all with the characteristic flower. Wild Blue Phlox blooms from April to June.

Identification   A loose cluster of pale blue-purple, red-purple, or white flowers, borne on a somewhat sticky stem with broad, lance-shaped leaves. Height: 10–20". Flowers ¾–1½" wide, with a narrow tube and 5 petal lobes flaring at right angles; style atop the ovary is about as long or longer than its 3 branches. Leaves broadly lance-shaped, 1–2" long, without stalks.

Habitat   Rich woods and fields.

Range   Minnesota, Quebec, and Vermont south to South Carolina, Alabama, and E. Texas.

182

Families and Their Members

185

Glossary

Alternate
Arranged singly along a
stem, not in opposite pairs.

Anther
The tip of a stamen, containing
pollen in 1 or more pollen sacs.

Basal
At the base of a stem.

Beard
A fringelike growth on a petal.

Bilateral
Having identical left and right
sides.

Bract
A modified, often scalelike, leaf,
usually at the base of a flower or
fruit.

Calyx
Collectively, the sepals of a flower.

Clasping
Surrounding or partly surrounding
the stem.

Cleft leaf
A leaf divided at least halfway to
the midrib.

Compound leaf
A leaf made up of two or more
leaflets.

Corymb
A flower cluster with a flat top,
with the individual pedicels
emerging from the stem at
different points, blooming from the
edges toward the center.

Cyme
A branching flower cluster
blooming from the center toward
the edges, with the tip of the axis
always bearing a flower.

Duff
The partly decayed organic matter
of the forest floor.

Involucre
A whorl or circle of bracts beneath
a flower or flower cluster.

Leaflet
One of the leaflike parts of a
compound leaf.

Lip petal
The lower petal of some irregular
flowers.

186

Lobe
A segment of a cleft leaf or petal.

Node
The place on the stem where leaves or branches attach.

Opposite
Arranged in pairs along each side of a twig or shoot.

Ovary
The enlarged base of a pistil, containing the ovules, which will ripen into seeds.

Palmate
Arranged around a central point like fingers on a hand.

Pedicel
The stalk of an individual flower.

Pappus
A bristle, scale, or crown on seedlike fruits.

Pinnate
Arranged in two rows along an axis, like a feather.

Pistil
The female structure of a flower, consisting of stigma, style, and ovary.

Pollen
The grains containing the male germ cells.

Raceme
A long flower cluster with flowers blooming on small stalks from a common, central, larger stalk.

Sepal
One of the outermost series of flower parts, arranged in a ring outside the petals, usually green and leaflike.

Spadix
A dense spike of tiny flowers, usually enclosed in a spathe.

Spathe
A bract or pair of bracts, often large, enclosing the flowers.

Spike
An elongated cluster of stalkless flowers.

Spur
A tubular elongation of a petal or a sepal.

Stamen
A male structure of a flower, consisting of a filament and a pollen-bearing anther.

Stigma
The tip of a pistil, which receives the pollen.

Style
The stalklike column of a pistil.

Terminal
Borne at the tip of the main stem or shoot.

Tuber
A swollen, mostly underground stem with buds.

Umbel
A flower cluster with individual flower stalks growing from the same point, like the ribs of an umbrella.

Whorled
Arranged along a twig or shoot in groups of three or more at each node.

Index

Photographers
Craig Blacklock (99)
Les Blacklock (33)
Jean T. Buermeyer (39, 97, 115, 119, 135, 153, 159)
Sonja Bullaty (111)
Kent and Donna Dannen (183)
Jack Dermid (25)
Harry Ellis (35, 41, 47, 59, 89, 91, 95, 113, 117, 157, 175, 177, 179)
Mary W. Ferguson (167)
Richard B. Fischer (43, 67, 129, 147, 155)
Lois T. Grady (63, 65, 77, 83, 87)
Joseph Guinta (61)
Elizabeth Henze (53)
John A. Lynch (45, 57, 163)
Anne McGrath (93, 109, 169)

National Audubon Society Collection/Photo Researchers, Inc.
Ruth Leming (55)

C.W. Perkins (139)
Tim Reeves (27, 127, 149)
Dorothy M. Richards (101)
J.M. Rowland (121, 161)
Dr. Werner W. Schulz (31, 123)
Mary Shaub (29, 71, 151, 171, 181)

John Shaw (107)
John J. Smith (173)
Joy Spurr (133)
Alvin E. Staffan (37, 51, 73, 81, 85, 125, 131)
David M. Stone (75, 165)
Lynn M. Stone (49, 137, 141, 145)
Edo Streekman (143)
Larry West (103, 105)
D. Wilder (69)
Marilyn Wood/Photo Nats (79)

Cover Photograph
Rugosa Rose
by Jean T. Buermeyer

Title Page
Common Blue Violet
by Harry Ellis

Spread (22–23)
Fragrant Water Lily
by Paul Rezendes

Illustrators
Bobbi Angell (14–21, 28, 30, 32, 34, 36, 38, 40, 42, 46, 50, 54, 58, 70, 84, 90, 98, 100, 108, 112, 132, 144, 148, 154, 156, 164, 170, 172, 176, 180)
Robin Jess (26, 34, 52, 60, 62, 72, 82, 86, 110, 114, 136, 138, 140, 142, 146, 162, 182)

Dolores R. Santoliquido (24, 44, 48, 56, 64, 66, 68, 74, 76, 78, 80, 88, 92, 94, 96, 102, 106, 116, 120, 122, 124, 126, 128, 130, 134, 150, 152, 158, 160, 166, 168, 174, 178)
M. J. Spring (104)

Prepared and produced by Chanticleer Press, Inc.

Founding Publisher: Paul Steiner
Publisher: Andrew Stewart

Staff for this book:

Editor-in-Chief: Gudrun Buettner
Executive Editor: Susan Costello
Managing Editor: Jane Opper
Senior Editor: Ann Whitman
Natural Science Editor: John Farrand, Jr.
Associate Editor: David Allen
Assistant Editor: Leslie Marchal
Production: Helga Lose, Gina Stead
Art Director: Carol Nehring
Art Associate: Ayn Svoboda
Picture Library: Edward Douglas

Original series design by Massimo Vignelli.

All editorial inquiries should be addressed to:
Chanticleer Press
500 Fifth Avenue, Suite 3620
New York, NY 10110

To purchase this book or other National Audubon Society illustrated nature books, please contact:
Alfred A. Knopf, Inc.
1745 Broadway
New York, NY 10019
(800) 733-3000
www.randomhouse.com

NATIONAL AUDUBON SOCIETY

The mission of NATIONAL AUDUBON SOCIETY *is to conserve and restore natural ecosystems, focusing on birds, other wildlife, and their habitats for the benefit of humanity and the earth's biological diversity.*

One of the largest environmental organizations, AUDUBON has 550,000 members, 100 sanctuaries and nature centers, and 508 chapters in the Americas, plus a professional staff of scientists, educators, and policy analysts.

The award-winning *Audubon* magazine, sent to all members, carries outstanding articles and color photography on wildlife, nature, the environment, and conservation. Audubon also publishes *Audubon Adventures*, a children's newspaper reaching 450,000 students. Audubon offers nature education for teachers, families, and children through ecology camps and workshops in Maine, Connecticut, and Wyoming, plus unique, traveling undergraduate and graduate degree programs through *Audubon Expedition Institute*.

AUDUBON sponsors books, on-line nature activities, and travel programs to exotic places like Antarctica, Africa, Baja California, and the Galápagos Islands. For information about how to become an Audubon member, to subscribe to *Audubon Adventures*, or to learn more about our camps and workshops, please contact:

NATIONAL AUDUBON SOCIETY
Membership Dept.
700 Broadway, New York, NY 10003-9562
(800) 274-4201 or (212) 979-3000
http://www.audubon.org/

Familiar Flowers of
North America
Eastern Region

Alfred A. Knopf, New York